Usborne

Build your own
MONSTER TRUCKS
Sticker Book

Designed by Marc Maynard

Written by Simon Tudhope

Illustrated by Gong Studios

Contents

Monster trucks are pickup trucks modified by larger wheels, deeper suspension and lightweight bodywork. They have supercharged engines and four-wheel steering for sharp cornering. They race around obstacle courses and drive in freestyle events where they compete to perform the craziest stunts. So get into gear for some four-wheeled mayhem and turn the page!

Usborne Quicklinks

For links to websites where you can watch monster trucks in action, go to the Usborne Quicklinks website at **www.usborne.com/quicklinks** and enter the keywords '**monster trucks**'. Please follow the internet safety guidelines at the Usborne Quicklinks website. We recommend that children are supervised while on the internet.

Lightning Strike

The race champion is back to defend its crown. With an engine adapted from a Top Fuel dragster, it blasts off ramps and tears around corners. Can lightning strike twice? You'd better believe it!

STATISTICS

▲ **Racing:** ██████████ 10
▲ **Freestyle:** █████ 5
▲ **Popularity:** ████████ 8
▲ **Toughness:** ██████ 6
▲ **Driver:** Jim 'Striker' Dolan

Mutant Thing

This beast is built to survive the axle-snapping strain of deep mud pits. Sending water and dirt flying into the crowd, it plunges right down and out the other side.

STATISTICS

- **Racing:** 6
- **Freestyle:** 5
- **Popularity:** 6
- **Toughness:** 9
- **Driver:** Marty 'Hog' Moore

Razor

Meet the freestyle king of the ring. With bodywork designed to roll the truck back onto its wheels, Razor pulls off stunt combos that leave other trucks stranded.

STATISTICS

▲ **Racing:** 7
▲ **Freestyle:** 10
▲ **Popularity:** 9
▲ **Toughness:** 7
▲ **Driver:** Cherie 'Moxie' Jones

Red Menace

This big air specialist lands the longest jumps in the game. Hitting the ramp at maximum speed, the crowd holds its breath as it soars across the arena.

STATISTICS

- Racing: ██████████ 8
- Freestyle: ██████████ 8
- Popularity: █████████ 7
- Toughness: █████████ 7
- Driver: Ted 'Scorchin' Mason

Sparks

This truck's party piece is the double backflip. It launches off a near-vertical ramp and spins skywards like a five-ton firework.

STATISTICS

- ▲ **Racing:** 6
- ▲ **Freestyle:** 9
- ▲ **Popularity:** 10
- ▲ **Toughness:** 7
- ▲ **Driver:** Brad 'Sparky' Nelson

Cobra's Curse

Cobra's Curse is showing its power. With four-wheel drive and a supercharged engine, it can scale cars and buses on just its two back wheels.

STATISTICS
- ▲ Racing: 8
- ▲ Freestyle: 8
- ▲ Popularity: 6
- ▲ Toughness: 6
- ▲ Driver: Jason 'Mummy' Lee

13

Bulldog

Bulldog's been let off its leash! With an ear-splitting roar and a hardened-steel muzzle, it smashes right through an old trailer.

STATISTICS

- **Racing:** 5
- **Freestyle:** 7
- **Popularity:** 8
- **Toughness:** 10
- **Driver:** Luca 'Barkin' Ramone

14

Rusty

It'll take more than a broken axle to stop ol' Rusty! Pushing itself to the limit and beyond, this veteran truck just gets fixed up and ready for another run.

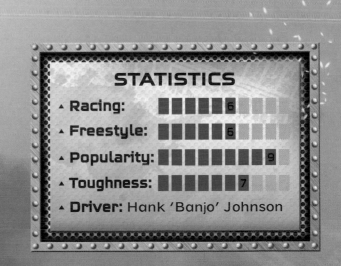

STATISTICS

- ▲ **Racing:** ▮▮▮▮▮▮ 6 ▯▯▯
- ▲ **Freestyle:** ▮▮▮▮▮▮ 6 ▯▯▯
- ▲ **Popularity:** ▮▮▮▮▮▮▮▮▮ 9 ▯
- ▲ **Toughness:** ▮▮▮▮▮▮▮ 7 ▯▯
- ▲ **Driver:** Hank 'Banjo' Johnson

Juggernaut

WARNING – this monster will flatten anything that gets in its way! The ground trembles as it thunders across the arena, looking for old cars to crush.

STATISTICS

▲ **Racing:** 5

▲ **Freestyle:** 7

▲ **Popularity:** 6

▲ **Toughness:** 9

▲ **Driver:** Bubba 'Digger' Ames

Kraken

Kraken's nailed one of the trickiest stunts in the business – the slap wheelie. It sails off the ramp, lands back wheels first, then – SLAP! – its front wheels hit the ground and bounce straight up.

STATISTICS

- ◄ Racing: 7
- ◄ Freestyle: 9
- ◄ Popularity: 9
- ◄ Toughness: 6
- ◄ Driver: Joe 'Swashbucklin' Hill

The Arena

The crowd is ready and the fireworks are lit – it's time for your trucks to fill the arena. Stick them wherever you like to make a mud-spraying, metal-crunching monster truck jamboree.

Glossary

- **axle:** the rod that a wheel turns on

- **big air:** a big, long jump

- **combos:** short for 'combinations'

- **four-wheel drive:** where the engine powers all four wheels (most pickup trucks are powered by their two back wheels). Useful on rough terrain when you can't rely on all the wheels having good contact with the ground.

- **four-wheel steering:** where the steering turns all four wheels (in most vehicles only the front two wheels turn). Monster trucks need this to perform sharp turns, because their wheels are so big.

- **freestyle:** a monster truck event where the trucks compete to perform the most impressive stunts

- **pickup truck:** a truck with no roof over its back end

- **supercharged engine:** an engine that uses compressed air to create more power

- **suspension:** a system that lets the wheels of a vehicle move up and down without moving the whole vehicle. Monster truck suspension uses pressurized gas rods, which are much longer and more durable than the metal springs used on most pickup trucks.

- **Top Fuel dragster:** the fastest type of drag racer. Built for maximum speed in a straight line.

Edited by Sam Taplin

Digital manipulation by Keith Furnival

The trucks, arenas and events represented in this book are not intended to replicate actual trucks, arenas or events.

First published in 2017 by Usborne Publishing Limited, 83-85 Saffron Hill, London EC1N 8RT, United Kingdom. usborne.com

Extra sticker

Extra sticker

Extra sticker

Sparks pages 10-11

Extra sticker

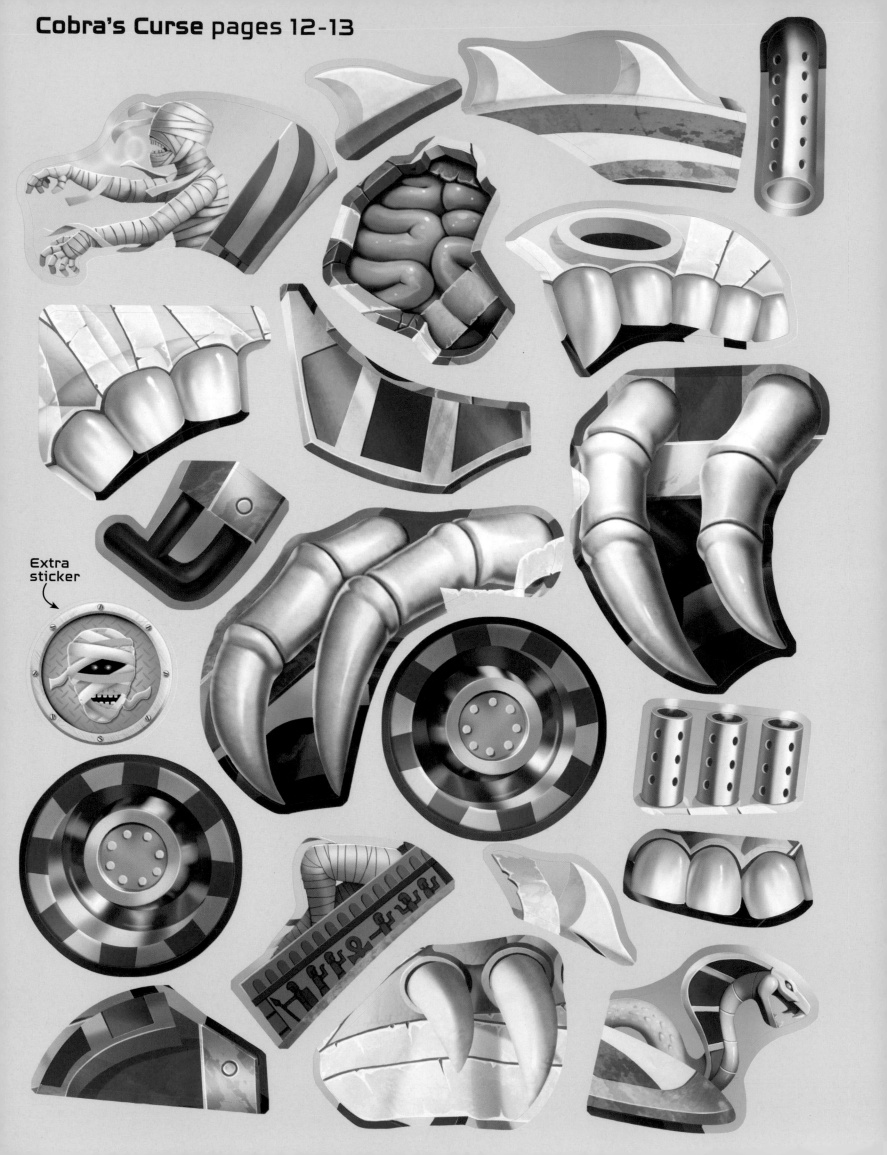

Extra sticker

Extra sticker

Extra sticker

Extra sticker

Extra sticker